The Jerilderie Letter
&
The Cameron Letter

by
Ned Kelly

Contents

The Jerilderie Letter   1
The Cameron Letter   21

The Jerilderie Letter

Dear Sir,

I wish to acquaint you with some of the occurrences of the present, past and future. In or about the spring of 1870 the ground was very soft; a hawker named Mr. Gould got his wagon bogged between Greta and my mother's house on the Eleven Mile Creek. The ground was that rotten it would bog a duck in places, so Mr. Gould had to abandon his wagon for fear of losing his horses in the spewy ground. He was stopping at my mother's awaiting finer or drier weather.

Mr. McCormack and his wife, hawkers also, were camped in Greta. The mosquitoes were very bad which they generally are with a wet spring to help them. Mr. Johns had a horse called Ruta Cruta, which although a gelding was as clever as Old Wombat or any other stallion at running horses away and taking them on his beat which was from Greta Swamp to the Seven Mile Creek, consequently he enticed McCormack's horse away from Greta. Mr. Gould was up early feeding his horses, heard a bell and seen McCormack's horse, for he knew the horse well. He sent his boy to take him back to Greta.

When McCormacks got the horse they came straight out to Gould and accused him of working the horse. This was false, and Gould was amazed at the idea. I could not help laughing to hear Mrs. McCormack accusing him of using the horse after him being so kind as to send his boy to take him from the Ruta Cruta and take him back to them. I pleaded Gould's innocence and Mrs. McCormack turned on me and accused me of bringing the horse from Greta to Gould's wagon to pull him out of the bog. I did not say much to the woman as my mother was present, but the same day when me and my uncle was cutting calves, Gould wrapped up a note and a pair of the calves' testicles and gave them to me to give them to Mrs. McCormack. I did not see her and gave the parcel to a boy to give to her when she would come. Instead of giving it to her he gave it to her husband. Consequently McCormack said he would summons me. I told him neither me nor Gould used their horse.

He said I was a liar, and he could welt me or any of my breed. I was about 14 years of age but accepted the challenge, and was dismounting when Mrs. McCormack struck my horse in the flank with a bullock's skin. It jumped forward and my fist came in collision with McCormack's nose, and caused him to lose his equilibrium and fall prostrate. I tied up my horse to finish the battle, but McCormack got up and ran to the Police Camp. Constable Hall asked me what the row was about. I told him they accused me and Gould of using their horse and I hit him, and would do the same to him if he challenged me. McCormack pulled me, and swore their lies against me.

I was sentenced to three months for hitting him and three months for the parcel, and bound to keep the peace for 12 months. Mrs. McCormack gave good substantial evidence as she is well acquainted with that place called Tasmania, better known as the Dervon or Van Diemens Land, and McCormack being a Policeman over the convicts and women being scarce released from that land of bondage and tyranny. They came to Victoria and are at present residents of Greta.

On the 29th March I was released from prison and came home. Wild Wright came to the Eleven Mile to see Mr. Gunn, stopped all night and lost his mare. Both him and me looked all day for her and could not get her. Wright, who was a stranger to me, was in a hurry to get back to Mansfield, and I gave him another mare, and he told me if I found his mare to keep her until he brought mine back. I was going to Wangaratta and saw the mare and I caught her and took her with me. All the Police and Detective Berrill seen her, as Martin's girls used to ride her about the town during several days that I stopped at Peter Martin's Star Hotel in Wangaratta. She was a chestnut mare, white face, docked tail, very remarkably branded (M) as plain as the hands on a town clock; the property of a Telegraph Master in Mansfield, he lost her on the 6th and gazetted her on the 12th of March. I was a prisoner in Beechworth Gaol until the 29th of March; therefore I could not have stole the mare.

I was riding the mare through Greta. Constable Hall came to me and said he wanted me to sign some papers that I did not sign at Beechworth concerning my bail bonds. I thought it was the truth. He said the papers was at the Barracks, and I had no idea he wanted to arrest me or I would have quietly rode away instead of going to the Barracks. I was getting off when Hall caught hold of me and thought to throw me, but made a mistake and came on the broad of his back himself in the dust. The mare galloped away, and instead of me putting my foot on Hall's neck and taking his revolver and putting him in the lockup, I tried to catch the mare. Hall got up and snapped three or four caps at me and would have shot me but the Colt's patent refused.

This is well known in Greta. Hall never told me he wanted to arrest me until after he tried to shoot me. When I heard the caps snapping I stood until Hall came close. He had me covered and was shaking with fear, and I knew he would pull the trigger before he would be game to put his hand on me. I duped and jumped at him, caught the revolver with one hand and Hall by the collar with the other. I dare not strike him or my sureties would lose the bond money. I used to trip him and let

3

him take a mouthful of dust now and again, as he was as helpless as a big goanna after leaving a dead bullock or horse.

I kept throwing him in the dust until I got him across the street to the very spot where Mrs. O'Brien's Hotel stands now. The cellar was just dug then; there was some brush fencing where the post and rail was taken down, and on this I threw the big cowardly Hall on his belly. I straddled him and rooted both spurs into his thighs; he roared like a big calf attacked by dogs and shifted several yards of fence. I got his hands at the back of his neck and tried to make him let the revolver go, but he stuck to it like grim death to a dead volunteer. He called for assistance to a man named Cohen, and (Thomas) Barnet, Lewis, Thompson, Jewitt and two blacksmiths who was looking on. I dare not strike any of them as I was bound to keep the peace, or I could have spread those curs like dung in a paddock.

They got ropes, tied my hands and feet, and Hall beat me over the head with his six chambered Colt's revolver. Nine stitches were put in some of the cuts by Doctor Hastings, and when Wild Wright and my mother came they could trace us across the street by the blood in the dust, and which spoiled the lustre of the paint on the gate-post of the Barracks. Hall sent for more Police and Doctor Hastings. Next morning I was handcuffed, a rope tied from them to my legs and to the seat of the cart and taken to Wangaratta. Hall was frightened I would throw him out of the cart, so he tied me whilst Constable Arthur laughed at his cowardice, for it was he who escorted me and Hall to Wangaratta.

I was tried and committed, as Hall swore I claimed the mare. The Doctor died, or he would have proved Hall a perjurer. Hall has been tried several times for perjury but got clear as this is no crime in the Police Force. It is a credit to a Policeman to convict an innocent man, but any mutt can pot a guilty one. Hall's character is well known about El Dorado and Snowy Creek, and Hall was considerably in debt to Mr. L. O'Brien and he was going to leave Greta. Mr. O'Brien seen no other chance of getting his money so there was a subscription collected for Hall. With the aid of this money he got James Murdoch, who was recently hung in Wagga Wagga to give false evidence against me but I was acquitted on the charge of horse-stealing. On Hall and Murdoch's evidence I was found guilty of receiving and got 3 years experience in Beechworth and Pentridges dungeons. This is the only charge ever proved against me. Therefore I can say I never was convicted of horse or cattle stealing.

My brother Dan was never charged with assaulting a woman, but he was sentenced to three months without the option of a fine, and one month and two pounds fine for damaging property by Mr. Butler, PM., a sentence there is no law to uphold. Therefore the Minister of Justice neglected his duty in that case, but there never was such a thing as justice in the English laws, but any amount of injustice to be had. Out of over thirty head of the very best horses the land could produce, I could only find one when I got my liberty. Constable Flood stole and sold most of them to the navvies on the railway line. One bay cob he stole and sold four different times. The line was completed and the men all gone when I came out, and Flood was shifted to Oxley.

He carried on the same game there. All the stray horses that was any time without an owner and not in the Police Gazette, Flood used to claim. He was doing a good trade at Oxley until Mr. Brown of the Laceby Station got him shifted as he was always running his horses about. Flood is different to Sergeant Steele, Strachan, Hall and the most of the Police, as they have got to hire cads and if they fail, the Police are quite helpless. But Flood can make a cheque single-handed. He is the greatest horsestealer, with the exception of myself and George King, I know of.

I never worked on a farm. A horse and saddle was never traced to me after leaving employment. Since February 1873 I

5

worked as a faller at Mr. J. Saunders and R. Rule's sawmills, then for Heach and Dockendorf. I never worked for less than two pound ten a week since I left Pentridge, and in 1875 or 1876 I was overseer for Saunders and Rule, Bourkes Water-holes Sawmills in Victoria. Since then I was on the Kings River. During my stay there I ran in a wild bull which I gave to Lydicher, a farmer. He sold him to Carr, a publican and butcher, who killed him for beef. Some time afterwards I was blamed for stealing this bull from James Whitty, of Boggy Creek.

I asked Whitty on Oxley Racecourse why he blamed me for stealing his bull. He said he had found his bull, and never blamed me, but his son-in-law, Farrell told him he heard I sold the bull to Carr. Not long afterwards I heard again I was blamed for stealing a mob of calves from Whitty and Farrell, which I knew nothing about. I began to think they wanted me to give them something to talk about. Therefore I started wholesale and retail horse and cattle dealing. Whitty and Burns not being satisfied with all the picked land on the Boggy Creek and King River, and the run of their stock on certificate ground free and no one interfering with them, paid heavy rent to the banks for all the open ground, so as a poor man could keep no stock. They impounded every beast they could get, even off Government roads.

If a poor man happened to leave his horse or a bit of poddy calf outside his paddock they would be impounded. I have known over 60 head of horses impounded in one day by Whitty and Burns, all belonging to poor farmers. They would have to leave their ploughing or harvest or other employment to go to Oxley. When they would get there, perhaps they would not have money enough to release them, and have to give a bill of sale or borrow money, which is no easy matter. Along with this sort of work, Farrell the Policeman stole a horse from George King and had him in Whitty and Farrell's paddocks until he left the force. All this was the cause of me and my stepfather George King taking their horses and selling them to Baumgarten and Kennedy.

The pick of them was taken to a good market and the culls were kept in Peterson's paddock, and their brands altered by me. Two was sold to Kennedy and the rest to Baumgarten who were strangers to me, and I believe, honest men. They paid me full value for the horses and could not have known they were stolen. No person had anything to do with the stealing and selling of the horses but me and George King. William Cooke, who was convicted for Whitty's horses, was innocent. He was not in my company at Peterson's.

But it is not the place of the police to convict guilty men, as it is by them they get their living. Had the right parties been convicted it would have been a bad job for the Police as Berry would have sacked a great many of them. Only I came to their aid and kept them in their billets and good employment and got them double pay, and yet the ungrateful articles convicted my mother and an infant, my brother-in-law and another man who was innocent, and still annoy my brothers and sisters. The ignorant unicorns even threaten to shoot myself, but as soon as I am dead they will be heels up in the muroo. There will be no more police required. They will be sacked and supplanted by soldiers on low pay in the towns, and special constables made of some of the farmers to make up for this double pay and expense.

It will pay the Government to give those people who are suffering innocence, justice and liberty. If not I will be compelled to show some colonial strategem which will open the eyes of not only the Victorian Police, and inhabitants, but also the whole British Army. No doubt they will acknowledge their hounds were barking at the wrong stump, and that Fitzpatrick will be the cause of greater slaughter to the Union Jack than Saint Patrick was to the snakes and toads in Ireland.

The Queen of England was as guilty as Baumgarten and Kennedy, Williamson and Skillion of what they were convicted for. When the horses were found on the Murray River I wrote a letter to Mr. Swanhill of Lake Rowan to acquaint the Auctioneer and to advertise my horses for sale. I brought some of them to that place, but did not sell. I sold some of them in Benalla, Melbourne and other places, and left the colony and became a rambling gambler.

Soon after I left there was a warrant for me and the Police searched the place and watched night and day for two or three weeks. When they could not snare me, they got a warrant against my brother Dan, and on the 15th of April Fitzpatrick came to the Eleven Mile Creek to arrest him. He had some conversation with a horse-dealer whom he swore was William Skillion. This man was not called in Beechworth besides several other witnesses, who alone could have proved Fitzpatrick's falsehood.

After leaving this man, he went to the house and asked was Dan in. Dan came out. I hear previous to this Fitzpatrick had some conversation with Williamson on the hill. He asked Dan to come to Greta with him, as he had a warrant for him for stealing Whitty's horses. Dan said "Allwright", and they both went inside. Dan was having something to eat. His mother asked Fitzpatrick what he wanted Dan for. The trooper said he had a warrant for him. Dan then asked him to produce it. He said it was only a telegram sent from Chiltern, but Sergeant Whelan ordered him to relieve Steele at Greta, and call and arrest Dan and take him in to Wangaratta next morning and get him remanded. Dan's mother said Dan need not go without a warrant unless he liked, and that the trooper had no business on her premises without some authority besides his own word.

The trooper pulled out his revolver and said he would blow her brains out if she interfered in the arrest. She told him it was a good job for him Ned was not there, or he would ram his revolver down his throat. Dan looked out and said, "Ned is coming now." The trooper being off his guard, looked out and when Dan got his attention drawn, he dropped the knife and fork, which showed he had no murderous intent, and slapped Heenan's

8

Hug on him, took his revolver and kept him there until Skillion and Ryan came with horses which Dan sold that night.

The trooper left and invented some scheme to say that he got shot, which any man can see is false. He told Dan to clear out, that Sergeant Steele and Detective Brown and Strachan would be there before morning. Strachan had been over the Murray trying to get up a case against him, and they would convict him if they caught him as the Stock Society offered an enticement for witnesses to swear anything and the Germans over the Murray would swear to the wrong man as well as the right.

Next day Williamson and my mother was arrested, and Skillion the day after, who was not there at all at the time of the row, which can be proved by 8 or 9 witnesses. The police got great credit and praise in the papers for arresting the mother of 12 children, one an infant on her breast, and those two quiet, hard working innocent men who would not know the difference between a revolver and a saucepan handle, kept them six months awaiting trial and then convicted them on the evidence of the meanest article that ever the sun shone on. It seems that the jury was well chosen by the Police as there was a discharged Sergeant amongst them, which is contrary to law. They thought it impossible for a Policeman to swear a lie, but I can assure them that it was by that means and hiring cads they got promoted. I have heard from a trooper that he never knew Fitzpatrick to be one night sober, and that he sold his sister to a chinaman, but he looks a young, strapping rather genteel man, more fit to be a starcher to a laundress than a policeman for to the keen observer he has the wrong appearance for a manly heart. The deceit and cowardice is too plain to be seen in the puny cabbage-hearted looking face.

I heard nothing of this transaction until very close on the trial, I being then over 400 miles from Greta. I heard I was outlawed and a hundred pound reward for me for shooting a trooper in Victoria and a hundred pound for any man that could prove a conviction of horse-stealing against me, so I came back to Victoria. I knew I would get no justice if I gave myself up. I enquired after my brother Dan and found him digging on Bullock Creek. I heard how the Police used to be blowing that they would not ask me to stand; they would shoot me first and then cry surrender. And how they used to rush into the house and upset all the milk dishes, break tins of eggs, empty the flour out of the bags onto the ground, and even the meat out of the cask and destroy all the provisions and shove the girls in front of them into the rooms like dogs, so as if anyone was there they would shoot the girls first. But they knew well I was not there, or I would have scattered their blood and brains like rain. I would manure the Eleven Mile with their bloated carcases, and yet remember there is not one drop of murderous blood in my veins.

Superintendent Smith used to say to my sisters, "See all the men I have out today? I will have as many more tomorrow and we will blow him into pieces as small as the paper that is in our guns." Detective Ward and Constable Hayes took out their revolvers and threatened to shoot the girls and children in Mrs. Skillion's absence. The greatest ruffians and murderers, no matter how depraved would not be guilt of such a cowardly action. This sort of cruelty and disgraceful and cowardly conduct to my brothers and sisters who had no protection, coupled with the conviction of my mother and those men certainly made my blood boil. I don't think there is a man born could have the patience to suffer it as long as I did, or ever allow his blood to get cold while such insults as these were unavenged. Yet in every paper that is printed I am called the blackest and coldest-blooded murderer ever on record. But if I hear any more of it I will not exactly show them what cold blooded murder is, but wholesale and retail slaughter - something different to shooting three troopers in self defence and robbing a bank.

I would have been rather hot blooded to throw down my rifle and let them shoot me and my innocent brother. They were

10

not satisfied with frightening my sisters night and day, and destroying their provisions and lagging my mother and infant, and those innocent men, but should follow me and my brother into the wilds where he had been quietly digging, neither molesting or interfering with anyone. He was making good wages, as the creek is very rich within half a mile from where I shot Kennedy.

I was not there long and on the 25th of October I came on Police tracks between Table Top and The Bogs. I crossed them and returning in the evening I came on a different lot of tracks making for the shingle hut. I went to our camp and told my brother and his two mates. Me and my brother went and found their camp at the shingle hut, about a mile from my brother's house. We saw they carried long firearms and we knew our doom was sealed if we could not beat those before the others would come. I knew the other party of Police would soon join them, and if they came on us at our camp they would shoot us down like dogs at our work, as we had only two guns.

We thought it best to try and bail those two up, take their firearms and ammunition and horses, and we could stand a chance with the rest. We approached the spring as close as we could get to the camp, as the intervening space being clear ground and no battery. We saw two men at the logs. They got up and one took a double-barrelled fowling piece, and fetched a horse down and hobbled him at the tent. We thought there were more men in the tent asleep, those outside being on sentry. We could have shot those two men without speaking, but not wishing to take their lives, we waited. McIntyre laid his gun against a stump and Lonigan sat on a log. I advanced, my brother Dan keeping McIntyre covered which he took to be Constable Flood, and had he not obeyed my orders, or attempted to reach for the gun or draw his revolver, he would have been shot dead.

When I called on them to throw up their hands McIntyre obeyed and Lonigan ran some six or seven yards to a battery of logs, instead of dropping behind the one he was sitting on. He had just got to the logs and put his head up to take aim when I shot him that instant, or he would have shot me, as I took him for Strachan, the man who said he would not ask me to stand, but would shoot me first like a dog. But it happened to be Lonigan, the man who, in company with Sergeant Whelan, Fitzpatrick and King the bootmaker, and Constable O'Day, tried to put a pair of handcuffs on me in Benalla, but could not, and had to allow McInnis the miller to put them on.

Previous to Fitzpatrick swearing he was shot, I was fined two pounds for hitting Fitzpatrick, and two pounds for not allowing five curs like Sergeant Whelan, O'Day, Fitzpatrick, King and Lonigan (who caught me by the privates and would have sent me to Kingdom Come only I was not ready) to arrest me. He is the man that blowed before he left Violet Town that if Ned Kelly was to be shot, he was the man would shoot him.

No doubt he would shoot me, even if I drew up my arms and laid down as he knew four of them could not arrest me single handed, not to talk of the rest of my mates. Either he or me would have to die. This he knew well, therefore he had a right to keep out of my road. Fitzpatrick is the only one I hit out of the five in Benalla; this shows my feeling towards him as he said we were good friends and even swore it. But he was the biggest enemy I had in the country with the exception of Lonigan, and he can be thankful I was not there when he took a revolver and threatened to shoot my mother in her own house.

It is not true I fired three shots and missed him at a yard and a half. I don't think I would use a revolver to shoot a man like him when I was within a yard and a half of him, or attempt to fire into a house where my mother, brothers and sisters was, and, according to Fitzpatrick's statement all around him. A man that is such a bad shot as to miss a man three times at a yard and a half would never attempt to fire into a house among a houseful of women and children while I had a pair of arms and a bunch of fives at the end of them. They never failed to peg out anything

12

they came in contact with, and Fitzpatrick knew the weight of one of them only too well as it run up against him once in Benalla and cost me two pound odd, as he is very subject to fainting.

As soon as I shot Lonigan he jumped up and staggered some distance from the logs with his hands raised and then fell. He surrendered, but too late. I asked McIntyre who was in the tent. He replied, "No one." I advanced and took possession of their two revolvers and fowling piece, which I loaded with bullets instead of shot. I asked McIntyre where his mates was. He said they had gone down the creek and he did not expect them that night. He asked me was I going to shoot him and his mates. I told him no; I would shoot no man if he gave up his arms and promised to leave the Force.

He said the Police all knew Fitzpatrick had wronged us, and he intended to leave the Force as he had bad health and his life was insured. He told me he intended going home, and that Kennedy and Scanlon were out looking for our camp and also about the other Police. He told me the N.S.W. Police had shot a man for shooting Sergeant Walling. I told him if they did they had shot the wrong man and I expect your band came to do the same with me. He said no, they did not come to shoot me, they came to apprehend me. I asked him what they carried Spencer rifles and breech-loading fowling pieces and so much ammunition for, as the Police was only supposed to carry one revolver and six cartridges in the revolver, but they had eighteen round of revolver cartridges each, three dozen for the fowling piece and twenty one Spencer rifle cartridges, and God knows how many they had away with the rifle. This looked as if they meant not only to shoot me, but to riddle me, but I don't know either Kennedy or Scanlon or him and had nothing against them. He said he would get them to give up their arms if I would not shoot them, as I could not blame them, they had to do their duty.

I said I did not blame them for doing honest duty, but I could not suffer them blowing me to pieces in my own native land. If they knew Fitzpatrick wronged us why not make it public and convict him, but no, they would rather riddle poor unfortunate creoles. But they will rue the day ever Fitzpatrick got among them. Our two mates came over when they heard the shot fired, but went back again for fear the Police might come to our camp while we were all away and manure Bullock Flat with us on arrival.

I stopped at the logs and Dan went back to the spring for fear the Troopers would come in that way, but I soon heard them coming up the creek. I told McIntyre to tell them to give up their arms. He spoke to Kennedy, who was some distance in front of Scanlon. He reached for his revolver and jumped off, on the off-side of his horse and got behind a tree. When I called on them to throw up their arms, Scanlon, who carried the rifle slewed his horse around to gallop away but the horse would not go, and as quick as thought, fired at me with the rifle without unslinging it and was in the act of firing again when I had to shoot him, and he fell from his horse.

I could have shot them without speaking but their lives was no good to me. McIntyre jumped on Kennedy's horse and I allowed him to go as I did not like to shoot him after he surrendered, or I would have shot him as he was between me and Kennedy. Therefore I could not shoot Kennedy without shooting him first. Kennedy kept firing from behind the tree. My brother Dan advanced and Kennedy ran. I followed him. He stopped behind another tree and fired again. I shot him in the armpit and he dropped his revolver and ran. I fired again with the gun as he slewed around to surrender. I did not know he had dropped his revolver - the bullet passed through the right side of his chest and he could not live - or I would have let him go. Had they been my own brothers I could not help shooting them or else let them shoot me, which they would have done had their bullets been directed as they intended them.

14

But as for handcuffing Kennedy to a tree, or cutting his ear off, or brutally treating any of them is a falsehood. If Kennedy's ear was cut off it was not done by me, and none of my mates was near him after he was shot. I put his cloak over him and left him as well as I could, and were they my own brothers I could not have been more sorry for them. This cannot be called wilful murder for I was compelled to shoot them, or lie down and let them shoot me. It would not be wilful murder if they packed our remains in, shattered into a mass of animated gore to Mansfield. They would have got great praise and credit as well as promotion, but I am reckoned a horrid brute because I had not been cowardly enough to lie down for them under such trying circumstances, and insults to my people.

Certainly their wives and children are to be pitied, but they must remember those men came into the bush with the intention of scattering pieces of me and my brother all over the bush, and yet they know and acknowledge I have been wronged and my mother and four or five men lagged innocent. And is my brothers and sisters and my mother not to be pitied also, who has no alternative, only to put up with the brutal and cowardly conduct of a parcel of big, ugly, fat-necked, wombat-headed, big-bellied, magpie-legged, narrow-hipped, splay-footed sons of Irish bailiffs or English landlords which is better known as officers of Justice or Victorian Police, who some calls honest gentlemen. But I would like to know what business an honest man would have in the Police, as it is an old saying, It takes a rogue to catch a rogue. And a man that knows nothing about roguery would never enter the Force and take an oath to arrest brother, sister, father or mother if required, and to have a case and conviction if possible.

Any man knows it is possible to swear a lie, and if a Policeman loses a conviction for the sake of swearing a lie, he has broke his oath. Therefore he is a perjuror either ways. A Policeman is a disgrace to his country, not alone to the mother that suckled him. In the first place he is a rogue in his heart, but too

15

cowardly to follow it up without having the Force to disguise it. Next, he is a traitor to his country, ancestors and religion, as they were all Catholics before the Saxons and Cranmore yoke held sway. Since then they were persecuted, massacred, thrown into martyrdom and tortured beyond the ideas of the present generation.

What would people say if they saw a strapping big lump of an Irishman shepherding sheep for fifteen bob a week or tailing turkeys in Tallarook ranges for a smile from Julia, or even begging his tucker? They would say he ought to be ashamed of himself and tar and feather him. But he would be a king to a Policeman, who for a lazy, loafing, cowardly billet left the ash corner and deserted the shamrock, the emblem of true wit and beauty to serve under a flag and nation that has destroyed, massacred and murdered their forefathers by the greatest of torture, such as rolling them down hill in spiked barrels, pulling out their toe and finger nails, and on the wheel and every torture imaginable.

More was transported to Van Deimens Land to pine their young lives away in starvation and misery among tyrants worse than the promised Hell itself. All of true blood, bone and beauty, that was not murdered on their own soil, or had fled to America or other countries to bloom again another day were doomed to Port MacQuarie, Toongabbie, Norfolk Island and Emu Plains, and in those places of tyranny and condemnation, many a blooming Irishman, rather than subdue to the Saxon yoke, were flogged to death and bravely died in servile chains, but true to the shamrock and a credit to Paddy's Land.

What would people say if I became a Policeman and took an oath to arrest my brothers and sisters and relations, and convict them by fair or foul means, after the conviction of my mother and the persecution and insults offered to myself and people? Would they say I was a decent gentleman? And yet a Policeman is still in worse and guilty of meaner actions than that. The Queen must surely be proud of such heroic men as the Police and Irish soldiers, as it takes eight or eleven of the biggest mud-crushers in Melbourne to take one poor little half starved larrikin to a watchhouse. I have seen as many as eleven, big and ugly enough to lift Mount Macedon out of a crab hole, more like the species of a baboon or gorilla than a man, actually come into a court house and swear they could not arrest one eight stone larrikin and them armed with battens and niddies. without some civilians' assistance, and some of them going to hospital from the effects of hits from the fists of the larrikin, and the Magistrate would send the poor little larrikin into a dungeon for being a better man than such a parcel of armed curs.

What would England do if America declared war and hoisted a green flag, as it is all Irishmen that has got command of her armies, forts and batteries? Even her very life guards and beef tasters are Irish. Would they not slew round and fight her with their own arms for the sake of the colour they dare not wear for years, and to reinstate it and raise old Erins isle once more from the pressure and tyrannism of the English yoke, which has kept it in poverty and starvation and caused them to wear the enemy's coat? What else can England expect?

Is there not big, fat-necked Unicorns enough paid to torment and drive me to do things which I don't wish to do, without the public assisting them? I have never interfered with any person unless they deserved it, and yet there are civilians who take firearms against me, for what reason I do not know unless they want me to turn on them and exterminate them without medicine. I shall be compelled to make an example of some of them if they cannot find no other employment. If I had robbed and plundered, ravished and murdered everything I met, young and old, rich and poor, the public could not do any more than take firearms and assist the Police as they have done, but by the light that shines, pegged on an ant-bed with their bellies opened, their fat taken out, rendered, and poured down their throats boiling hot will be cool to what pleasure I will give some of them. Any person aiding or harbouring or assisting the Police in any way whatever, or employing any person whom they know to be a detective or cad, or those who would be so depraved as to take blood money will be outlawed and declared unfit to be allowed human burial. Their property either consumed or confiscated and them, theirs and all belonging to them exterminated off the face of the earth. The enemy I cannot catch myself I shall give a payable reward for.

I would like to know who put that article that reminds me of a poodle dog, half clipped in the lion fashion, called Brooke E. Smith, Superintendent of Police. He knows as much about commanding Police as Captain Standish does about mustering mosquitoes and boiling them down for their fat on the backblocks of the Lachlan, for he has a head like a turnip, a stiff neck as big as his shoulders, narrow hipped and pointed towards the feet like a vine stake. If there is any one to be called a murderer regarding Kennedy, Scanlon and Lonigan, it is that misplaced poodle. He gets as much pay as a dozen good troopers, if there is any good in them, and what does he do for it? He cannot look behind him without turning his whole frame. It takes three or four Police to keep sentry while he sleeps in Wangaratta, for fear of body snatchers. Do they think he is a superior animal to the men that has to guard him? If so, why not send the men that gets big pay and reckoned superior to the common Police after me and you shall soon save the country of high salaries to men that is fit for nothing else but getting better men than himself shot, and sending orphan children to the industrial school to make prostitutes and cads of them for the Detectives and other evil disposed persons.

Send the high paid and men that received big salaries for years in a gang by themselves after me, as it makes no difference to them, but it will give them a chance of showing whether they are worth more pay than a common trooper or not. I think the public will soon find they are not only in the road of good men but obtaining money under false pretences. I do not call McIntyre a coward, for I reckon he is as game a man as wears the Jacket, as he had the presence of mind to know his position directly he was spoken to, and only foolishness to disobey.

It was cowardice that made Lonigan and the others fight. It is only foolhardiness to disobey an outlaw, as any Policeman or other man who do not throw up their arms directly as I call on them, knows the consequences, which is a speedy dispatch to Kingdom Come. I wish those men who joined the Stock Protection Society to withdraw their money and give it and as much more to the widows, and orphans and poor of Greta district, where I spent and will again spend many a happy day, fearless, free and bold, as it only aids the Police to procure false witnesses and go whacks with men to steal horses and lag innocent men. It would suit them far better to subscribe a sum and give it to the poor of their district, and there is no fear of anyone stealing their property, for no man could steal their horses without the knowledge of the poor.

If any man was mean enough to steal their property, the poor would rise out to a man and find them if they were on the face of the earth. It will always pay a rich man to be liberal with the poor and make as little enemies as he can, as he shall find if the poor is on his side, he shall lose nothing by it. If they depend on the Police they shall be drove to destruction, as they cannot and will not protect them. If duffing and bushranging were abolished, the Police would have to cadge for their living. I speak from experience, as I have sold horses and cattle innumerable, and yet eight head of the culls is all ever was found. I never was interfered with whilst I kept up this successful trade.

I give fair warning to all those who has reason to fear me to sell out, and give 10 pounds out of every hundred towards the widow and orphan fund and do not attempt to reside in Victoria but as short a time as possible after reading this notice, neglect this and abide by the consequences, which shall be worse than the rust in the wheat in Victoria or the druth of a dry season to the grasshoppers in New South Wales.

I do not wish to give the order full force without giving timely warning, but I am a widow's son outlawed, and my orders must be obeyed.

Edward Kelly.

The Cameron Letter

Through the Cameron letter the KellyGang tell their story in their own words.

The text is from the original held by the Public Records Office of Victoria as transcribed for Max Brown. Donald Cameron MLA was a Victorian politician who called upon Berry, the Prime Minister of Victoria for an inquiry into the conduct of the police after the Mansfield Murders in November 1878. Berry relpied that if he would hold an inquiry if he had information that, '..difficulties were interposed, by want of proper organisation among the police ..' The KellyGang took him at his word and wrote to Cameron. He did nothing about it but pass the letter on to Berry. It would seem that Berry saw no political advantage in taking the matter any further.

"Dear Sir,

Take no offence if I take the opportunity of writing a few lines to you, wherein I wish to state a few remarks concerning the case of Trooper Fitzpatrick against Mrs Kelly, W. Skillion, and W. Williamson, and to state the facts of the case to you. It seems to me impossible to get justice without I make a statement to someone that will take notice of it, as it is no use in me complaining about anything that the police may choose to say or swear against me, and the public in their ignorance and blindness will undoubtedly back them up to their utmost. No doubt I am now placed in very peculiar circumstances and you might blame me for it, but if you knew how I have been wronged and persecuted you would say I cannot be blamed. In April last an information was (which must have come under your notice) sworn against me for shooting Trooper Fitzpatrick, which was false, and my Mother with an infant baby and brother-in-law and another neighbour was taken for aiding and abetting and attempting to murder him, a charge of which they are as purely innocent as the child unborn.

During my stay in the King River I run in a wild bull which I gave to Lydicker who afterwards sold him to Carr and he killed him for beef. Some time afterwards I was told I was blamed for stealing this Bull from Whitty. I asked Whitty on Moyhu Racecourse why he blamed me for stealing his bull and he said he had found the bull, and he never blamed me for stealing him. He said it was - who told film that I stole the bull. Some time afterward I heard again I was blamed for stealing a mob of calves from Whitty and Farrell, which I never had anything to do with, and along with this and other talk, I began to think they wanted something to talk about. Whitty and Burns not being satisfied with all the picked land on King River and Boggy Creek, and the run of their stock on the Certificate ground free, and no one interfering with them paid heavy rent for all the open ground so as a poor man could not keep any stock and impounded every beast they could catch even off Government roads, if a poor man happened to leave his horse or bit of poddy calf outside his paddock, it would be impounded, I have known over 60 head of horses to be in one day impounded by Whitty and Burns, all belonging to poor men of the district. They would have to leave their harvest or ploughing and go to Oxley and then perhaps not have money to release them and have to give a bill of sale or borrow the money, which is no easy matter, and along with all this sort of work --- the policeman stole a horse from George King and had him in Whitty and Jeffrey's paddock until he left the Force and this was the cause of me and my stepfather George King stealing Whitty's horses and selling them to Baumgarten and those other men, the pick of them was sold at Howlong and the rest was sold to Baumgarten who was a perfect stranger to me and I believe an honest man.

No man had anything to do with the horses but me and George King. William Cooke who was convicted for Whitty'.s horses had nothing to do with them, nor was he ever in my company at Peterson's the German at Howlong. The brand was altered by me and George King and the horses sold as strait. Any man requiring horses would have sought them the same as those men and would have been potted the same and I consider Whitty ought to do something towards the release of those innocent men, otherwise there will be a collision between me and him as I can to his satisfaction prove.

I took J. Welsh's black mare and the rest of the horses, which I will prove to him, in next issue, and after those horses had been found and the row being over them, I wrote a letter to Mr Swannell of Lake Rowan to advertise my horses for sale, as I was intending to sell out. I sold them afterwards at Benalla and the rest in New South Wales and left Victoria as I wished to see certain parts of the country and very shortly afterwards as there was a Warrant for me, as I since hear the Police Sergeant Steele, Straughan and Fitzpatrick and others searched the Eleven Mile and every other place in the district for me and a man named Newman, who had escaped from the Wangaratta Police for months before the I5th of April.

Therefore it was impossible for me to be in Victoria, as every schoolboy knows me, and on the 15th of April, Fitzpatrick came to the Eleven Mile and had some conversation with Williamson who was splitting on the hill, seeing my brother and another man, he rode down and had some conversation with this man whom he swore was William Skillion. This man was not called in Beechworth as he could have proved Fitzpatrick's falsehood as Skillion and another man was away after horses at this time, which can be proved by eight or nine witnesses. The man who the troopers swore was Skillion can prove Williamson's innocence besides other important evidence, which can be brought on the prisoner's behalf. The trooper after speaking to this man rode to the house and Dan came out. He asked Dan to go to Greta with him. Dan asked him what for and he said he had a warrant for him for stealing Whitty's horses. They both went inside, Dan was having something to eat.

The trooper was impatient and Mrs Kelly asked him what he wanted Dan for, he said he had a Warrant for him. Dan said produce your Warrant and he said he had none, it was only a telegram from Chiltern. Mrs Kelly said he need not go unless he liked without a warrant. She told the trooper he had no business on her premises without some authority besides his own word. He pulled out his revolver, and said he would blow her brains out if she interfered in the arrest. Mrs Kelly said, if Ned was here, he would ram the revolver down his throat. To frighten the trooper Dan said, Ned is coming now. The trooper looked around to see if it was true. Dan dropped the knife and fork which showed he had no murderous intention clapped Heenans Hug on him, took his revolver and threw him and part of the door outside and kept him there until Skillion and Ryan came with horses which Dan sold that night, the trooper left and invented some scheme to say he got shot, which any man can see it was impossible for him to have been shot.

He told Dan to clear out that Sergeant Steele or Detective Brown would be there before morning, as Straughan was over the Murray trying to get up a case against Dan and the Lloyds as the Germans over the Murray would swear to anyone and they will lag you guilty or not. Next day Skillion, Williamson and Mrs Kelly, with an infant were taken and thrown into prison and were six months awaiting trial and no bail allowed and was convicted on the evidence of the meanest man that ever the sun shone on. I have been told by Police that he is hardly ever sober, also between him and his father they sold his sister to a chinaman, but he seems a strapping and genteel looking young man and more fit to be a starcher to Laundry than a trooper, but to a keen observer, he has the wrong appearance to have anything like a clear conscience or a manly heart. The deceit is too plain to be seen in the White Cabbage hearted looking face, I heard nothing of this transaction until very close on the trial I being then over 400 miles from Greta.

I heard that I was outlawed and 100 pound reward for me in Victoria and also hundreds of charges of Horse Stealing was against me, beside shooting a trooper. I came into Victoria and enquired after my brother and found him working with another man at Bullock Creek. Heard how the police used to he blowing that they would shoot me first and then cry Surrender. How they used to come to the house where there was no one there but women and Superintendent Smith used to say. See all the men I have today, I will have as many more tomorrow and blow him into pieces as small as the paper that is in our guns and they used to repeatedly rush into the house revolver in hand upset milk dishes, empty the flour out on the ground, break tins of eggs, and throw the meat out of the cask on to the floor, and dirty and destroy all the provisions, which can be proved and shove the girls in front of them into the rooms like dogs and abuse and insult them.

Detective Ward and Constable Hayes took out their revolvers and threatened to shoot the girls and children, while Mrs Skillion was absent, the oldest being with her, the greatest murderers and ruffians would not be guilty of such an action. This sort of cruelty and disgraceful conduct to my brothers and sisters who had no protection coupled with the conviction of my Mother and those innocent men certainly made my blood boil as I don't think there is a man born could have the patience to suffer what I did. They were not satisfied with frightening and insulting my sisters night and day and destroying their provisions and lagging my Mother with an infant baby and those innocent men, but should follow me and my brother who was innocent of having anything to do with any stolen horses, into the wilds, where he had been quietly digging and doing well, neither molesting or interfering with anyone and I was not there long and on the 25th October I came on the tracks of police horses, between Table Top and the Bogs, I crossed there and went to Emu Swamp and returning home came on more police tracks making for our camp.

I told my mates and me and my brother went out next morning and found police camped at the Shingle Hut with long

25

fire arms and we came to the conclusion our doom was sealed unless we could take their fire-arms, as we had nothing but a gun and a rifle if they came on us at our work or camp. We had no chance only to die like dogs as we thought the country was woven with police and we might have a chance of fighting them if we had firearms, as it generally takes 40 to one. We approached the Spring as close as we could get to the camp, the intervening space being clear. We saw two men at the Log, they got up and one took a double barrel fowling piece and one drove the horses down and hobbled them against the tent and we thought there was more men in the tent, those being on sentry. We could have shot those two men, without speaking, but not wishing to take life we waited. McIntyre laid the gun against the stump and Lonigan sat on the log.

I advanced, my brother Dan keeping McIntyre covered. I called on them to throw up their hands McIntyre obeyed and never attempted to reach for his gun or revolver, Lonigan ran to a battery of logs and put his head up to take aim at me, when I shot him, or he would have shot me, as I. knew well, I asked who was in the tent, McIntyre replied no one. I approached the camp and took possession of their revolvers and fowling piece which I loaded with bullets instead of shot. I told McIntyre I did not want to shoot him or any man that would surrender. I explained Fitzpatrick's falsehood which no policeman can be ignorant of. He said he knew Fitzpatrick had wronged us but he could not help it. He said he intended to leave the Force on account of his bad health, his life was insured, the other two men who had no firearms came up when they heard the shot fired and went back to our camp for fear the police might call there in our absence and surprise us on our arrival.

My brother went back to the Spring and I stopped at the Log with McIntyre. Kennedy and Scanlan came up, McIntyre said he would get them to surrender if I spared their lives as well as his. I said I did not know either him Scanlan or Kennedy, and had nothing up against them, and would not shoot any of them, if they gave up their firearms and promised to leave the Force, as it was the meanest billet in the world. They are worse than cold-blooded murderers and hangmen. He said he was sure they would never follow me any more. I gave them my word that I would give them a chance. McIntyre went up to Kennedy, Scanlan behind with a rifle and a revolver. I called on them to throw up their hands. Scanlan slewed his horse around to gallop away, but turned again and as quick as thought fired at me with the rifle and was in the act of firing again, when I shot him.

Kennedy alighted on the off side of his horse and got behind a tree and opened hot fire. McIntyre got on Kennedy's horse and galloped away. I could have shot him if I choose as he was right against me but rather than break my word I let him go. My brother advanced from the Spring, Kennedy fired at him and ran as he found neither of us was dead. I followed him, he got behind another tree and fired at me again. I shot him in the armpit as he was behind the tree, he dropped his revolver and ran again and slewed round and I fired with the gun again and shot him through the right chest as I did not know that he had dropped his revolver and was turning to surrender. He could not live or I would have let him go. Had they been my own brothers, I could not help shooting them or else lie down and let them shoot me, which they would have done had their bullets been directed as they intended them. But as for handcuffing Kennedy to a tree or cutting his car off or brutally treating any of them, is a cruel falsehood.

If Kennedy's ear was cut off, it has been done since I put his cloak over him and left him as honourable as I could and if they were my own brothers I could not be more sorry for them, with the exception of Lonigan I did not begrudge him what bit of lead he got as he was the beastliest meanest man that I had any account against for him. Fitzpatrick, Sergeant Whelan, Constable Day and King, the Bootmaker, once tried to hand-cuff me at Benalla and when they could not Fitzpatrick tried to choke me, Lonigan caught me by the privates and would have killed me but was not able. Mr McInnes came up and I allowed him to put the hand-cuffs on when the police were bested.

This cannot be called wilful murder for I was compelled to shoot them in my own defence or lie down like a cur and die. Certainly their wives and children are to he pitied, but those men came into the bush with the intention of shooting me down like a dog, yet they know and acknowledge I have been wronged. And is my Mother and infant baby and my poor little brothers and sisters not to be pitied more so, who has got no alternative only to put up with brutal and unmanly conduct of the police who have never had any relations or a Mother or must have forgot them. I was never convicted of horse stealing. I was once arrested by Constable Hall and 14 more men in Greta, and there was a subscription raised for Hall, by persons who had too much money about Greta, in honour of Hall arresting Wild Wright and Gunn, Wright and Gunn were potted and Hall could not pot me for horse stealing, but with the subscription money he gave 20 pounds to James Murdoch, who has recently been hung in Wagga Wagga and on Murdoch's evidence, I was found guilty of receiving, knowing to be stolen, which I, Wright, W. Ambrose, J. Ambrose and W. Hatcher and W. Williamson and others can prove I was innocent of knowing the Mare to be stolen, and I was accused of taking a hawker by the name of McCormack's horse to pull another hawker named Ben Gould out of a bog.

Mr Gould got up in the morning to feed his horses, seen Mr McCormack's horse, and knew he had strayed and sent his man with him about two miles to where McCormack was camped in Greta. Mr and Mrs McCormack came out and seen the waggons bogged and accused him of using the horse. I told Gould that was for his good nature. Mrs McCormack turned on me and accused me for catching the horse for Gould, as Gould knew that he was wicked and could not catch him himself. Me and my uncle was cutting and branding calves and Ben Gould wrapped up a pair of testicles, wrote a note and gave it to me to give to Mrs McCormack. McCormack said he would fight me I was then 14 years of age, I was getting off my horse and Mrs McCormack hit the horse, he jumped forward and my fist came in collision with Mr McCormack's nose who swore he was standing 10 yards away from another man and the one hit knocked the two men down. However ridiculous the evidence may seem, I received three months or 10 pounds, for hitting him and 3 months for delivering the parcel and bound to the peace for 12 months.

At the time I was taken by Hall and his 14 assistants, therefore I dare not strike any of them as Hall was a great cur. And as for Dan he never was tried for assaulting a woman. Mr Butler, P.M., sentenced him to 3 months without the option of a fine and one month or two pounds fine for wilfully destroying property, a sentence which there is no law to uphold, and yet they had to do their sentence and other prosecutors. Mr D. Goodman since got 4 years for perjury concerning the same property. The Minister of justice should enquire into this respecting their sentence and he will find a wrong jurisdiction given by Butler P.M. on the 19th of October 1877 at Benalla and these are the only charges was ever proved against either of us, therefore we are falsely represented. The reports of bullets having been fired into the bodies of the Troopers after death is false and the Coroner should he consulted. I have no intention of asking mercy for myself or any mortal man or apologising, but wish to give timely warning that if my people do not get justice and those innocents released from prison and the police wear their uniform, I shall be forced to seek revenge of everything of the human race for the future, I will not take innocent life, if justice is given, but as the police are afraid or ashamed to wear their uniforms, therefore every man's life is in danger.

As I was outlawed without any cause and cannot be no worse, and have but once to die, and if the public do not see justice done, I will seek revenge for the name and character which has been given to me and my relations while God gives me strength to pull a trigger. The witness which can prove Fitzpatrick's falsehood can be found by advertisement and if this is not done immediately horrible disasters shall follow, Fitzpatrick shall be the cause of greater slaughter to the rising generation than St Patrick was to the snakes and frogs in Ireland, for had I robbed, plundered, ravished and murdered everything I met, my character could not be painted blacker than it is at pre-

29

sent, but thank God my conscience is as clear as the snow in Peru, and as I hear a picked jury amongst which was a discharged Sergeant of Police, was empanelled on the trial and David Lindsay who gave evidence for the Crown is a Shanty Keeper having no licence and is liable to a heavy fine and keeps a book of information for the police and his character needs no comment for he is capable of rendering Fitzpatrick any assistance he required for a conviction as he could be broke any time Fitzpatrick chose to inform on him. I am really astonished to see Members of the Legislative Assembly led astray by such articles as the Police, for while an outlaw reigns their pocket swells, Tis double pay and country girls –

By concluding, as I have no more paper unless I rob for it, if I get justice I will cry a go. For I need no lead or powder to revenge my cause. and if words be louder, I will oppose your laws. With no offence. (Remember your Railroads), and a sweet good bye from,

EDWARD KELLY
A Forced Outlaw

Also from Benediction Books ...
Wandering Between Two Worlds: Essays on Faith and Art
Anita Mathias
Benediction Books, 2007
152 pages
ISBN: 0955373700

Available from www.amazon.com, www.amazon.co.uk

In these wide-ranging lyrical essays, Anita Mathias writes, in lush, lovely prose, of her naughty Catholic childhood in Jamshedpur, India; her large, eccentric family in Mangalore, a sea-coast town converted by the Portuguese in the sixteenth century; her rebellion and atheism as a teenager in her Himalayan boarding school, run by German missionary nuns, St. Mary's Convent, Nainital; and her abrupt religious conversion after which she entered Mother Teresa's convent in Calcutta as a novice. Later rich, elegant essays explore the dualities of her life as a writer, mother, and Christian in the United States-- Domesticity and Art, Writing and Prayer, and the experience of being "an alien and stranger" as an immigrant in America, sensing the need for roots.

About the Author

Anita Mathias is the author of *Wandering Between Two Worlds: Essays on Faith and Art.* She has a B.A. and M.A. in English from Somerville College, Oxford University, and an M.A. in Creative Writing from the Ohio State University, USA. Anita won a National Endowment of the Arts fellowship in Creative Nonfiction in 1997. She lives in Oxford, England with her husband, Roy, and her daughters, Zoe and Irene.

Visit Anita at http://www.anitamathias.com, and on http://theoxfordchristian.blogspot.com, her Christian blog; http://wanderingbetweentwoworlds.blogspot.com/, her personal blog, and http://thegoodbooksblog.blogspot.com, her literary and writing blog.

The Church That Had Too Much
Anita Mathias
Benediction Books, 2010
52 pages
ISBN: 9781849026567

Available from www.amazon.com, www.amazon.co.uk

The Church That Had Too Much was very well-intentioned. She wanted to love God, she wanted to love people, but she was both hampered by her muchness and the abundance of her possessions, and beset by ambition, power struggles and snobbery. Read about the surprising way The Church That Had Too Much began to resolve her problems in this deceptively simple and enchanting fable.

About the Author

Anita Mathias is the author of *Wandering Between Two Worlds: Essays on Faith and Art.* She has a B.A. and M.A. in English from Somerville College, Oxford University, and an M.A. in Creative Writing from the Ohio State University, USA. Anita won a National Endowment of the Arts fellowship in Creative Nonfiction in 1997. She lives in Oxford, England with her husband, Roy, and her daughters, Zoe and Irene.

Visit Anita at http://www.anitamathias.com, and on http://theoxfordchristian.blogspot.com, her Christian blog; http://wanderingbetweentwoworlds.blogspot.com/, her personal blog, and http://thegoodbooksblog.blogspot.com, her literary and writing blog.